STRESS-BUSTING FOR CHILDREN

(The best kept secret since Father Christmas)

Rita Sparks

evolutionary
pathways

First Published in Great Britain in 2004
by evolutionary pathways
P.O. Box 8121, Billericay CM11 1WZ

ISBN No 0-9548195-0-0

Typeset by Quintessence, Billericay CM12 9DF
Printed in Great Britain by Creative Print Design, Harmondsworth UB7 0LW

Dedicated to children everywhere.

Our future is in your hands.

*This book places the power of loving
guidance into the hands of those who
care the most – parents.*

*Within these pages will be found a unique
method to help you endow your children
with gifts beyond price: to be happy,
harmonious and enriched on
their journey through life.*

CONTENTS

Introduction

Many people may not realise the extent to which unconscious stress affects the lives of children, even those in the most warm and loving of home environments. It is the main reason for bad behaviour and various other problems too. If the psyche of a child is out of kilter it can result in a variety of symptoms such as bedwetting, breathing difficulties, nightmares, fears and phobias, aggression, timidity and a great many more uncomfortable conditions.

This book explains how unconscious stress forms in a child's mind through the process of repression, and how it adversely affects their behaviour from childhood right through into adult life. But, more importantly, it provides parents with the remedy to eliminate that stress from their children and explains how this can be achieved in a safe, uncomplicated way by using a method which is not only rewarding but also fun for both parent and child. The process is perfectly natural, and involves no more than the time-honoured pleasure of story-telling.

CHAPTER 1

Repression

Have you ever noticed how amazingly clever Mother Nature is? She has a way of organising things so that by the time we get to be parents we have lost touch with the feelings of our childhood. With the hand of kindness she has drawn a veil of mist over those stomach-churning moments of agony that we experienced all those years ago. Like the time when we were made to stand up and recite our four times table in front of the whole class, or the gut-wrenching disappointment when we weren't chosen to play in the school team, or, (factor 6 on the "squirm" scale) talking in class and being made to stand in the corridor outside the classroom, silently praying that the Head wouldn't choose that moment to pass by and see you there.

As adults we can generally recall events from our past, and perhaps remember a little of the emotion too, but the bulk of those childhood emotions has very efficiently been hidden away deep in our subconscious minds. Mother Nature mercifully buried those feelings for a very good reason: to protect the child. It's a wonderful defence mechanism called repression and it is unique to children. The process of repression allows children to exist in an adult world, for without it they would find life extremely difficult. Repression spontaneously diverts harsh reality away from a child's tender mind and ensures that their minds survive intact to adulthood. Indeed, it is the safety mechanism of repression that makes children *appear* to be so resilient, so adaptable to change. But appearances can be deceptive. The effect of subconscious repression inevitably changes behaviour, sometimes quite drastically, giving rise to symptoms that can be detrimental to the child's well-being.

Adults are not able to repress, much as we would like to when we're in the midst of emotional turmoil, because the process of repression ceases to occur round about the age of 16. The adult mind will use other means to deal with emotional pain. Denial, disavowal, or even amnesia in the case of extreme emotional trauma, but only children have that built in by-pass system of repression: it is not on the adult menu.

You would be amazed at the things that get buried in a child's mind, truly amazed!! I think that, in order to illustrate this point, a little exercise would be appropriate here.

I'd like you to imagine that you've just bought a beautiful new car. You've saved up for years, spent hours choosing the model, the colour, the extras, and you've just taken delivery of your sleek new machine that attracts such admiring glances as you drive around the neighbourhood. Then I come along and say to you:-

"Give me the keys to your car please. My friend wants to borrow it for a while".

What would your response be? (I am putting you on your honour here and trusting you to be absolutely truthful.) Would you say?

(a) "O.K. Here you are. Tell your friend to have a good time with my beautiful new car."

(b) "No. This is mine. Tell your friend to go and buy his own"

(c) "What... You must be kidding!"

(d) Something else

Whichever way you responded, I'm sure that you would feel justified in having an opinion, having the right to decide for yourself what happens to your car.

Now let's look at a little boy, 5 years of age, who has just got a shiny new bicycle from Father Christmas. It might seem at first glance that this is a very simple method for a child to obtain what he desires - just write to Father Christmas and ask him to bring it for you. Wrong! It's more complicated than that. For the past few months this little chap has been lovingly blackmailed into being extra good. "Father Christmas doesn't come to visit naughty boys you know, only ones that are really good. He knows whether you've washed behind your ears or not, what time you go to bed, whether you've been helping nicely or getting in mummy's way and being a nuisance."

It seems to the child that this jolly festive character gets everywhere. He knows everything about you, even what you think and feel.

So, the bike didn't come easy. Our little hero has been eating up his cabbage and spinach for weeks and he's been as good and helpful as he can be. He even smiled bravely and tried not to mind when auntie Mary kissed him and suffocated him in a bear hug. And now he's been rewarded. He's got his dream bike that he rides around the garden, and sometimes in the park too if a grown-up is with him and then everybody can see it and admire it and know how good he must have been to get such a super bicycle for Christmas. His face is beaming with pleasure and pride as he rides about and people stop to tell him what a lucky boy he is.

Then comes the day in the Christmas holidays when mum's long-lost friend comes to visit and brings her little boy with her. A little cherub whom our hero doesn't know from Adam and, whilst the mums chat in the kitchen, the boys are told to "play nicely" in the garden. When the inevitable squabble breaks out over who gets to ride the shiny new bike, the mothers then have to work out the fairest way to please everyone. The visiting mother will probably try to distract her little treasure by pointing out all of the other things he can play with, whilst our hero's mother, not wanting her visitors to think her child selfish, will encourage him to release his strangle-hold on the bicycle and to "share nicely and take turns".

May I ask you at this point how you'd be feeling if someone who is twice your size were now prising your fingers from around your tightly clutched car keys whilst reading you the riot act on how to share nicely and not be selfish?

Getting back to junior, he really doesn't think it a good idea to have his space invaded by a strange child who wants to take his bike, so he gets really angry and begins to lash out with fury. His mother is now beginning to worry about the effect his tantrum is having on her friend's view of *her*, imagining her friend thinking of our hero "what a spoiled brat" or, of her, "she can't even control her own 5 year old". So the mother feels she should now make a stand and insist on her little boy's co-operation, perhaps going so far as to tearing the bicycle away from him and giving it to the other child. At the same time she is probably telling our little hero not to be angry, or selfish, or naughty, or uncooperative, or anti-social, or all of those things.

Let's try to imagine what emotions are coursing through that little boy. He's certainly angry: one look at his screwed up red face can verify that!!! He's no doubt confused too. All he did was to hold on to his own bike and now all hell's broken loose. His mother is shouting at him, and might even have administered a slap by now. In fact, there's a strong possibility that he'll end up in his room until he "calms down and learns how to behave."

How are you doing with the car keys? You're now in a situation where they've been wrested from your grasp and you're having to suffer the indignity of seeing a stranger drive off in your car: none too carefully by the looks of things. Are you feeling calm, sociable, and co-operative? No?

Admit it. It's much more likely that you'd feel angry, really angry. But don't worry; I have the remedy to put everything right. All I need tell you is .....

"Stop that at once. How dare you be angry".

There! How does that feel? Better now?

One thing is for sure; you are not likely to say "What a good idea. I'll stop feeling angry right now. Why didn't I think of that before? I could have saved myself a lot of tears and frustration"

In fact you're far more likely to feel even angrier at my suggestion, because my words are showing you that I don't understand your rage, or, worse still, that you're not entitled to feel it.

Well, the young man in our illustration can't "feel to order" any more than you can. However, he has a secret weapon to protect him, one which adults do not possess and, bless him, he doesn't even know it. This is where Mother Nature steps in and "hey presto", most of the horrible feelings get buried deep in the child's subconscious mind instead of registering in the brain. It works rather like a safety valve. The child will naturally experience *some* of the emotion and will no doubt express this with tears and tantrums, but when the danger level is reached on the safety valve, those overwhelming feelings of rage, hate, frustration and powerlessness, feelings that he just cannot deal with, will bypass his conscious experience and, in the blink of an eye, be whisked away and buried in the very deepest part of his sub-conscious. But something else will be buried with it too. Guilt ! After all, his mother is cross with him for expressing anger, so therefore he must be bad. In addition to this, that momentary hatred of his mother will produce even more guilt, lots of it, because she is, at this stage of his life, one of the most important people in his world and the person that cares for him the most. What is more, he really didn't mean to lash out and hit the visiting child - it somehow just happened and now he's hurt the other little boy and has managed to upset just about everyone. More guilt for that store of repressions!

As parents we tread a very fine line. We want

our children to grow up to be thoughtful, well-balanced and sociable and therefore we need to apply direction and discipline to enable them to achieve this. No one likes a little monster that runs wild, or a spiteful bully. It is essential that bad behaviour is checked, but in steering our children along all the right paths towards acceptance by society we inevitably cause them to form repressions. It cannot be helped. *There is no other way.* Most of us love our children enough to play the baddie sometimes by insisting on a certain standard of behaviour. Our job as parents is not to strive to be at the top of our children's popularity list, but to have the courage to draw the line in the sand and create boundaries. Children feel so much safer when there are guidelines clearly marked out for them, and the security that they find within this discipline provides them with a clear framework and solid foundation on which they can build their individuality and creativity as they grow.

So it is indeed fortunate that, for the sake of a child's emotional survival, there are many negative feelings that never register into a child's intellect. Mother Nature immediately comes to the rescue by putting a seal around the pain, rather like a bubble-wrap, and hides it out of sight deep in the sub-conscious. Every time there is an event that causes an excess of emotion another bubble is formed, and each bubble is frozen at the age that the child was when the event occurred. For instance, inside one bubble is a 3 year old who lost sight of mummy in the supermarket and panicked, and inside another is a 7 year old who didn't get invited to the party that all his friends went to, and inside that one is a 10 year old who was bitten by a dog.

The illustration of the little boy with the bicycle describes how an actual event can cause a repression to take place, but repression also happens as a result of a child's imagination. If a child is told, "there's a monster behind the curtain" then immediately there is an image of the monster in the child's mind. The face, the fangs, the claws; every blood-curdling detail. It is not necessary for the child to actually see the monster; just the belief in its existence is enough to cause terror. A child's physiological response to imagined fear is exactly the same as if face to face with the monster. The racing heart, the laboured breathing, the perspiration, the shaking. If you have ever woken a child from a nightmare, you'll know what I mean. Whilst they were in that dream, for them, it really was real.

Whilst looking at "belief", let's also look at "mistaken belief" because that is yet another factor that can cause repression to take place. In the "letters from readers" section in a magazine a mother told of how her little girl reacted in a totally unpredictable way to a family discussion. They were planning a holiday and the mother was saying something like " we'll fly to Florence and have 3 days sightseeing and then we'll fly on to Venice....." No-one was taking much notice of the little girl in the corner until her sobs became urgent and, after much coaxing to tell why she was so upset, she said "you're all going away without me and you're going to leave me here alone because I don't know how to fly." It might have amused the family, but she really believed that if she couldn't fly like Tinkerbell in the story of Peter Pan then her family would fly off and abandon her. I'm quite sure that, within seconds, the little girl would have been scooped up into comforting arms, reassured, covered with kisses and given an explanation about a big silver aeroplane that will take all of the family to visit lovely places. Far too late, unfortunately, to have prevented a repression taking place because, in a split second, that overwhelming terror of being abandoned and unloved (albeit untrue) would have zoomed into the repression store and no amount of love or explanation would be able get it out again: the one way door closed firmly behind it.

So one can see clearly that almost anything can cause a repression to take place. Being bullied at school, arguments with friends, scary teachers, angry parents, growly dogs, creepy films – absolutely anything.

Even wonderful things that will enrich a child's life can, *unconsciously*, be viewed by a child as a threat to its security. A child who has always been the focus of it's parent's attention just does not see a new baby brother or sister as a potential playmate. It may seem that way on the surface, but be assured, there would be a lot of repression taking place underneath. That is why, on a conscious level, the child might really love the new arrival and even help to care for it, but might also start to develop a change in behaviour such as bed-wetting, nightmares or stuttering as a result of the unconscious anxieties that have become repressed and consequently give rise to such symptoms.

Few people who have read "Cider with Rosie" could fail to be moved by Laurie Lee's poignant account of his childhood as he describes the devastation of being usurped from the warmth of his mother's bed by a younger sibling.

To illustrate the point, it would be interesting to put ourselves in an equivalent adult situation so that we can begin to relate to a child's unconscious fears.

Imagine a husband announcing to his wife

"Darling I really love you. In fact I'm so happy to be married to you that I'm going to the wife-shop tomorrow and I'm going to get another wife. Then I'll bring her home to live with us, and we can all live really happily together. She'll be company for you and you'll be able to go shopping together and have lots and lots to talk about. Won't that be fun?" Ouch!

Any wife would have difficulty dealing with the impact of such a statement, even though she is a grown up and has developed adult resources. How much more painful for a child having to deal with a rival appearing on the scene! Thank goodness for the sagacity of Mother Nature in preventing such despair from ever touching the conscious minds of children. One can only applaud her infinite wisdom.

What might seem perfectly straightforward to one child can create a mountain of fear in another. I remember being terrified at the age of 5 by seeing a boy wearing a Mardi gras head whilst I was playing in the local swing park with my sisters. All of the other children thought it was great fun but I took to my heels and ran for my life. On the other hand, having witnessed family violence from a very early age, I was bewildered when a visiting child ran out of our house screaming when my parents starting fighting and the pots and pans were flying through the air. I thought you just ducked!

But isn't it wonderful to know how protected our children are? It is, without doubt, children's ignorance of true reality that safeguards their sanity, which is why a child who, having been beaten black and blue by a violent parent will cry for that same parent whilst being patched up in the casualty ward. It is one of the reasons why children don't tell when they're being abused by the very people who should be protecting them, because the actual truth, the real horror of a situation, is mercifully, compassionately, buried in a deep and secret place far away from the conscious mind.

Of course one of the main reasons that Mother Nature so effectively keeps reality well away from a child's conscious mind is because we are all driven by the strongest primeval instinct of all – the will to survive! It makes perfect sense when you think about it. If a child were to experience the true intensity of an emotional experience, and then were to outwardly express the anger and hatred that it gives rise to, particularly towards the hand that feeds him, then his very existence could be in jeopardy. He could perish. Well, Mother Nature is not going to permit that to happen. Much safer to allow just *some* of the emotion to register in the child's mind whilst, at the same time, burying the really intense, potentially destructive stuff.

So, getting back to the bicycle incident, when junior was stomping up the stairs to his room, not only was he thinking "I hate her", but he meant it – he really meant it! And when his fury reached danger level, the safety valve of repression immediately sprang into action and that powerful concentration of emotion was buried in a place where the child was, and still is, totally unaware of it. Isn't Nature wonderful?

CHAPTER 2

How repression affects our behaviour

You might imagine that, having successfully locked away that overpowering and unexpressed emotional energy into a safe and secret place, it would be nice to believe that the child will now grow into adulthood without a care in the world, totally unaffected by the pain of unpleasant childhood experiences.

If only that were so! Unfortunately life does not work that way. The reality is that, although the repressions are stored safely away from the conscious mind of the child, they still play an **unconscious** part in the child's behaviour and will continue to do so for the rest of the child's life and all through adulthood. Every time the child is under stress those bubbles will start to shake about and give the child an almost physical sense of anxiety. Rather like butterflies in the tummy in most cases. In extreme instances, more like a punch in the solar plexus.

As a child approaches the age of 16 or so, and adulthood looms, the process of repression decreases and then stops altogether. That one-way door into the repression store is now firmly bolted, trapping those bubbles, all of which will become more and more agitated with time. They will spend forever trying to attract our attention by swirling around and digging us in the ribs from time to time, in the vain hope that we will be persuaded to look within ourselves to find what the problem is. Some hopes! This would be a rare occurrence indeed.

If we have a physical pain – well that's easily dealt with. We'll try a few remedies and if they don't relieve us of the pain, we'll take ourselves off to our doctor. We willingly give the medical profession the responsibility of putting us right, perhaps sometimes even resorting to surgery. And pain is always the first thing that alerts us to the fact that something isn't right within our body.

But what about emotional pain? Pain that takes the form of nervousness, phobias, panic attacks, depression, lack of confidence, neurosis, aggression, shyness? How often do we look within ourselves to find the cause? Sadly, it seems to be the last place that most of us think of looking.

Take a moment to think about it. Logically. Realistically. Where else could the answer be found? Feelings are not things that drift about in the air, giving us the opportunity to decide whether we'd like to entertain them or not. They are coming from somewhere within, that's the only place they can possibly be found. Within each one of us.

The problem is that we find it difficult to accept that fact because we feel that we *ought* to be feeling fine. Life is not treating us too badly. There are no monsters hiding behind the curtain or under our beds. That spider that makes us squeal with horror isn't carrying a machine gun. There is no rational reason whatsoever to feel afraid. So why do so many of us spend so much time living a fear-based existence? Fear of rejection, fear of failure, fear of not being clever enough, attractive enough, loved enough, rich enough, secure enough?

So many human beings are merely existing rather than living because they are inhibited by their innermost feelings, feelings that, however hard they try, they just cannot understand. How could they? How could anyone possibly understand something that they have absolutely no knowledge of? Those unexplainable negative feelings were accumulated *unconsciously* by the child that the adult used to be. That is why adult reason, logic, and all the intelligence in the world cannot make any sense of such feelings, because the child that the adult used to be, at the time the emotion was repressed, did not have the resources that the adult now has.

By the time we reach adulthood we have gained so much: experience of life, education, integrity, discernment and, most importantly, the ability to reason. Ever tried to reason with a 5 year old?

Inside those bubbles of repressed emotion there is absolutely no sense of time. For instance, inside that bubble is the belief that you are still 3 years old, and inside that one you are 5 years old. The interior of those bubbles has no idea that you are all grown up now and they are still performing the task that they were put there to accomplish in the first place – to protect the child from the harshness of reality at all costs, to keep the child's sanity intact.

Let us look now at the formation of a repression in order to understand how it works. It falls into three parts:

- the event itself
- the physical aspect
- the emotional aspect

At the time a repression takes place, it splinters. Let's take as an example a little girl who wets her knickers on her first day at school. There's a puddle forming around her feet, which the other children have noticed (and we all know how unkind children can be to each other). The poor little mite is so embarrassed: she just wants the ground to open up and swallow her. Whilst it all depends on the emotional state of the child, let us suppose, to illustrate the process, that 30% of each one of those three aspects is experienced by the child. That is 30% of knowing what is happening, 30% of the physical discomfort and 30% of the emotional trauma: it all registers in the child's intellect and is experienced and dealt with by the child. But as the child's level of emotional trauma rises, the safety valve then becomes activated and the other 70% is repressed: meaning that 70% of the knowledge and details of the event; 70% of the physical discomfort and 70% of the emotional pain all automatically bypasses the brain and represses by burying itself directly into the subconscious.

Emotion is the vehicle of repression. Without it a repression would not take place. So you could in fact have a situation where 100% of the knowledge of an event itself registers in the consciousness of the child and 100% of the emotion represses into the subconscious. This, of course, would lead us, as adults, to assume that we know everything there is to know about our past. After all, we have excellent memories and can recall, in vivid Technicolor detail, exactly what happened at a particular childhood event. But what about the anguish that never registered into our awareness, the part that bypassed the brain (and therefore the memory) and went straight into the subconscious? It is because we are totally oblivious to this that explains why we are able to look back in time and believe, really sincerely believe, that we were unaffected by certain events which took place in our childhood, little knowing that the emotion connected to a particular event is in fact still trapped deep within us.

Whenever an adult is in a situation where they feel stressed, it is not just the anxiety of the current situation that is so upsetting. It is also because this anxiety is made worse by the addition of those bubbles of negative energy that are squirming around in the repression store.

If those bubbles were not there, we would then have the ability to look at and to respond to situations with adult eyes and consequently make rational and adult decisions. But those repressions don't allow that to happen because, burdened with the child's excess emotion, we are seeing it all through the eyes of the frightened child whose overspill of anxiety became trapped inside. Therefore every decision we make in our adult lives is *unconsciously* influenced by the 3 year old who lost sight of mummy in the supermarket, and the 5 year old who tangled with mummy over the bicycle, and the 7 year old who didn't get to go to the party and, bearing in mind that we all have hundreds of these bubbles of repression, it is hardly surprising that we sometimes feel and act like children, particularly when under pressure. It would be interesting to watch very carefully the next time you see an adult under stress; during an argument perhaps. Watch the body language. The way the hands go onto the hips, the chin juts forward, the voice gets louder and louder. Maybe they'll flounce off if they are losing the battle. Reminiscent of kinder-garten do you think?

Whether we recognise it or not, it is a fact that, as adults, our bubbles will run our lives for us: they become our "drivers" because that trapped negative energy inside of the bubbles will be constantly trying to discharge. For our own sakes, even though it might seem perverse, our subconscious minds will actually endeavour to attract people and situations into our lives in order for us to have the opportunity to discharge the negative energy and thereby resolve a particular issue. We cannot progress without offloading this negativity, so the subconscious will continue to show us, over and over again, the problems that must be resolved. For example, in extreme cases where most of the repressed material is due to violence, women will be attracted to men who have violent characters. It seems irrational and they certainly wouldn't make such a selection consciously. However, sad as it might be, the fact remains that it is all too often the case. It is as though the subconscious is holding up a mirror and saying to us "hey, look at this, then look within, that's our problem. Recognise it?" It sounds very much as though our subconscious is being a bit unkind, does it not, but, paradoxically, it is behaving with infinite wisdom. It wants the very best for us: it yearns for harmony and peace, but there is no way that the subconscious can achieve that serenity whilst there is so much agitation from those blockages of negative energy. But we inevitably misinterpret the signals and develop repetitive behaviour, simply replicating the same emotional exercises over and over again. We make identical mistakes. We choose the wrong partners, make the wrong decisions in the hope that "this time it will turn out differently". But it doesn't change, because inside of ourselves we still contain that repressed negative energy.

Whilst it is the *subconscious* mind's job to bring emotional turmoil to the attention of the conscious mind, it is, however, the *conscious* mind's job to do something about it. Unfortunately, the usual remedy is to reach for the tranquillisers or antidepressants to ease the disquiet that so often seems to have arrived from nowhere and for absolutely no reason. This does no more than mask a problem we do not recognise and therefore cannot resolve or move on from. As a result the process of maturity is inhibited.

It would be so simple if each bubble of repressed emotion could be easily identified: it would certainly make a lot more sense. Then you could reasonably assume that you hate being in enclosed spaces because you were shut in a cupboard at the age of 5. That is a plausible assumption, and might well be the reason. But if it is, it's not the only one. You see, in most cases, it is the *sum total* of all of the negative bubbles trapped within us that is constantly striving to discharge and that sum total of energy will attach itself to almost anything. So when we feel emotional pressure as adults, for whatever reason, it activates all of the hidden childhood material too, causing us to behave in a very "over the top" manner, reacting in a way that is far beyond that which the situation warrants. Well of course that is bound to happen. It is not just an adult that is responding to the situation: it is an adult plus the buried emotions inside each childhood bubble of repression.

So our natural defence mechanism comes into play and we cope by avoiding situations which might stir up our bubbles of anxiety. As a result we spend our lives compromising, doing our best not to put ourselves in a position where we would feel nervous or less than confident. What a waste!

So, what can be done to change things?

CHAPTER 3

It doesn't have to be that way

In my professional role people seek my help in resolving a variety of emotional problems and it is difficult to generalise because their stories are so incredibly varied. Most have tried many things over many years to keep their bubbles quiet, to quell that feeling of disquiet deep within, so that they are able to cope. Reliance on alcohol is probably one of the most common ways in which people try to ease their anxieties, along with anti-depressants and tranquillisers. It is heart-breaking to increasingly read that children are now being dosed with mini-sized versions of such chemical coshes.

The saddest thing is that the effect of all these props is merely an illusion. It might feel as though they have taken away our troubles, but when the effect of the chemicals wears off, we are right back where we started. I am not saying that anti-depressants do not have their uses, because they do. I know of cases where they have been taken for a short period of time to help someone over a particularly nasty blip in their lives and have proved to be extremely effective. Regrettably, that is not always the case.

Hard drugs, too, are becoming more and more prevalent amongst youngsters and some who have experimented with mind-altering substances have frightened the lives out of themselves because, far from achieving the feeling of well-being which they are seeking, they become paranoid and suffer terrifying hallucinations, not to mention risking the prospect of permanent damage to their brain cells.

Would it surprise you to know that each adult who comes to me for help, for whatever reason, will receive exactly the same course of treatment? Each client is guided through precisely the same process. Bubble popping!

A typical example would be a mother who will come to me and say, something like "I don't know what's wrong with me. I have a husband who loves me very much, we have three wonderful children, we have no financial worries and we live a great life-style. But I can't stop crying. And I don't know why. I've got nothing to cry about.

"The thought of meeting new people terrifies me and I know, although my husband is being very patient with me, that I'm getting in the way of his career because I can't entertain and be a good hostess like the other wives. Any form of socialising sends me into a cold sweat and it's agony to spend an evening with my husband's colleagues. I can't think of one intelligent thing to say. Yet I know that I am an intelligent person.

I keep panicking for no reason. I actually had to be helped out of the school hall at my son's speech day last week – I just turned to jelly and started shaking and crying. I was so nervous that I couldn't breathe. I was fighting for breath and thought that I might be having a heart attack.

Thank goodness my friend was there to help me, but I missed my son's presentation and he was so disappointed. That was the last straw! Now I've decided to do something about it. Can you help me?"

Yes. I can. This lady is suffering from that which the whole human race is suffering from. It is quite simply a question of degrees and she just happens to have more repressions than most. But we all have them; every one of us. There are no exceptions. We could not have survived to the age of sixteen without them. Those hidden bubbles, filled with repressed emotion, are trying to get her to notice them, and the only way that they can do that is by swirling around and making a nuisance of themselves. It's as though they are saying "Hey, look down here, we've got a problem. We're uncomfortable. We're all trapped in here and we can't get out".

My adult clients are treated by taking them through the process of analysis, which is not the subject of this book. Suffice to say that I act as a catalyst for each client to reach his or her repressions in order to release the trapped childhood emotion. And then each client will change. They will change in remarkable ways. It is truly a pivotal point of their lives.

And they change, not because I want them to, nor because they are trying to, but because a fundamental change takes place within their psyche when the pressure of their childhood emotional trauma is removed, when the negative energy accumulated in their early years is discharged. Clients do not receive counselling from me, nor advice. We do not need to deal with anything at all in relation to their everyday adult problems. Each client is guided to achieve the unloading of the excess emotional baggage that they have, without realising it, been dragging through their lives with them. Baggage that they collected before the age of 16. Without exception.

Imagine a milk bottle that is three quarters filled with milk that has gone rock hard. And let us say that this rocky substance represents all of the childhood repressions that were collected before the age of 16, and it is stuck there forever. Now, let us say that adult trauma is represented by water. So, we have an argument with our partner and water is poured into the bottle and lies on top of the rocky matter. Then we get behind with our mortgage and a little more water is added. When we have a good day, well, some of the water gets poured out again. It comes and goes, flowing with life's ups and downs, but it is always on top of what lies beneath. What all this boils down to is the fact that we have very little leeway to play with before the water reaches the top of the bottle, because the depth of the rocky substance below restricts the space for it. That's when the water spills over and becomes a problem. That's the point when we feel that we are losing control. That's the point where our emotions begin to fluctuate out of all proportion and unsettle us. We find that we're either doing something that we don't want to do, (like having panic attacks, phobias, smoking, drinking alcohol) or we're not doing something that we do want to do (like saying how we really feel, applying for that job we've always wanted, asking that girl out to dinner). We're being bossed around and dominated by that negative trapped energy and therefore will never reach our full potential.

Adult analysis is the process whereby we progressively clear out all of the rocky material and, when that is gone, the water in the top of the bottle goes all the way down to the bottom. Look at how much leeway we have now!! Our capacity to deal with life is enormous. Life would have to be extremely tough to get that water even half way up the bottle now, let alone make it overflow.

So we don't waste time by looking at, or dealing with, the symptoms that are erupting at the top of the bottle. We are only interested in the cause. In other words, what was repressed up to the age of 16. When the cause is removed, the symptom simply diminishes and eventually disappears. It sounds too good to be true, doesn't it, but I assure you that it is exactly how it works. I can honestly say that the only reason that I listen to a prospective client's problems when they first come to see me is because I'm polite. But, at the risk of sounding harsh, it is almost irrelevant for me to even know why someone comes to see me in the first place because, once we start work, all that we will be doing is bubble popping. Once those childhood bubbles have surfaced and dissolved, so the client's symptoms will melt away too.

Once this is accomplished that person will *automatically* gain the strength and resilience to deal with whatever life has in store for them. It is a momentous turning point. At long last they actually take control of their lives because, after treatment, they will be living their life from an adult perspective. They will never go back to being the nerve-wracked person whom I first met: once those bubbles get out they can't get back in. That person is over sixteen now and the adult mind cannot repress. Cause and effect! Remove the cause and the effect is also removed. Root out the cause of the discomfort, the unconscious negative energy, and the fear and anxiety, whatever form it takes, will disappear.

But children are different and that is the point

of this book. There is no need for them to be burdened with excess emotion as they make their way through life. Remember, the repression door doesn't get bolted until the age of about 16, so we can sneak out some of the pressure before that happens. And we can do it in such a way that the children aren't even aware that it's happening. All we need to use is the magic that all children possess in abundance – imagination!

CHAPTER 4

The best kept secret since Father Christmas

Let me tell you how this all came about.

I have been treating children for many years and it is necessary to use a totally different method from that used for adults, because children can still repress. In my consulting room I have a stress-meter and I am often astounded at the level of stress that some children have bottled up inside them. Children are brought to me for many reasons. Some have panic attacks, some have been bullied, some have dreadful nightmares, some are bullies and are extremely aggressive, others are particularly timid, some wet the bed, some have speech problems, some have breathing problems and some are just generally lacking in confidence. The list of problems is endless.

Over the years I have constructed a series of exercises that help to remove their unconscious stress. I do not **ever** look at how the stress got there – I would not want the child to become aware of an occurrence or experience that was so strong that it repressed, because if I were instrumental in bringing a child's repression up to the surface, it would only repress back down again and, even worse, take me with it because, added to their problem would be the pressure of being dragged off to see me - a complete stranger. So another way had to be found.

Deal with it symbolically! That was the answer and it was so simple! Remember how the little girl who couldn't fly thought that she would be abandoned? Well, that was because the subconscious cannot tell the difference between what is real and what is not real. It merely reacted to the situation, even though the situation wasn't real. She only *imagined* that it was. The power of the imagination is wondrous; especially the power of a child's imagination, and it is this power that can liberate your children and allow them to become the people that they were born to be; that will help enable them to reach their fullest potential throughout the rest of their lives.

It all started with a little girl who was too young for me to treat. She was only 5 years old and had been wetting the bed ever since she'd stopped wearing nappies. She wouldn't settle, would get up from bed three or four times every night and was generally very nervous. She had also just started school and it was becoming increasingly difficult to get her through the school gates. Her mother was very disappointed when I told her that I couldn't help because the child was so young.

And then I had an idea. I explained to her about the visualisation exercises that I do with older children and asked her if she could do them with her child if I wrote them down and showed her what to do.

To help ensure that the child's imagination and attention would be maintained, I carefully wove a fairy story involving a Princess around those same visualisation exercises. That night the mother read to her child "The Princess" story, which incorporated the exercises, and then put her to bed. The little girl stayed there all night, and, what is more, woke up in a dry bed the next morning for the very first time in her life. In addition the problems with school were eliminated and she completely overcame her nervousness.

My experience told me to expect a positive result, but I was amazed at the speed with which the desired effect was achieved. It taught me a very valuable lesson. That the child's mother obtained a better result than I, as a therapist, could ever have achieved because the work was done in the comfort and the security of the child's home and was done by the person she trusted the most: her mother. And most of all, there was absolutely no pressure on the child because I had told the mother the secret:

DO NOT TELL YOUR CHILD WHY YOU ARE READING HER A "DIFFERENT" KIND OF STORY

Had she said to her little girl "I'm going to read you a special kind of story to stop you wetting the bed", then it would have added to the child's stress and put more pressure on her to control something that she was clearly not capable of controlling.

The work that parents will be able to undertake with the help of this book is carried out from a totally different direction. We are going to be in the business of removing your children's stress, not adding to it. So we do not look at the symptom. We do not address the symptom. We do not even mention the symptom. We totally ignore it. Because, **whatever** that symptom might be, it will lessen when we reduce the tension created by the bubbles of repressed emotion. Cause and effect. It always comes back to cause and effect.

We are going to pop the children's bubbles symbolically – they'll never know, and they won't feel a thing! All they will know is that mummy or daddy sometimes reads them a bedtime story about a Princess or, in the case of boys, a story about a Captain in the Rangers.

CHAPTER 5

So let's get to work

Chapters 6 and 7 are scripts for you to read to your child: one for girls and one for boys. It is essential that you read through them thoroughly to familiarise yourself with them and, most importantly, the "variations" section and the questions and answers. Practice with the scripts until you can flow with the essence of the work, until it becomes as natural to you as reading Cinderella.

Now here's the tricky bit. In order to achieve the visualisation needed for success it will be necessary for your child to keep his (or her) eyes closed all the time. Let us suppose you are going to read the Princess story to your little girl. You could say something like "Would you like to have a special story tonight. One that you can join in?" You can tell her that she can be in the story too and wear a beautiful princess dress. Not many little girls could resist that! Or maybe "Let's play pretend. Close your eyes because it's easier to make up pretend pictures that way."

All that I can say is that you are the parents and you know your child better than anyone else. (Having said that, it might be useful for you to know that some mums and dads have resorted to bribery, just to get things going. That's fine: whatever it takes!)

Whilst on the subject of closed eyes, you will notice during some parts of the story that your child's eyes will be darting about all over the place underneath her eyelids. This is because she's watching the action in her mind's eye, just as we all experience rapid eye movement whilst we are dreaming.

It is important that your child participates and interacts with you during the story; that you get responses from her, and I have indicated the places where she should respond. If she doesn't, just repeat the question until she does respond: sometimes she'll just nod or smile, but the more she joins in, the better the result. Some children become very animated whilst doing the work: they are such a joy to watch and they are obviously having a great time.

Have fun while you are working with your child and don't take it all too seriously. If your child persists in opening her eyes all the time; well, it's no big deal, try again some other time. She might just not be in the mood to co-operate. There is only one golden rule, and I cannot emphasise it enough

NEVER TELL YOUR CHILD WHY YOU ARE READING HER THE STORY.

It would only bring her attention to her problem and put more pressure on her. The reason that you carry out these exercises truly does have to be the best kept secret since Father Christmas.

NOTE: For obvious reasons it would be a good idea to cover this book with wrapping paper or something similar in order to keep from your child any idea that you are dealing with their stress problems.

Take your time doing the work. The slower the better and with plenty of pauses. It gives children more opportunity to conjure up the pictures in their minds.

Results from your work will vary from child to child, but there have been some amazing outcomes. One little boy who used to have dreadful attacks of breathlessness did "The Captain" exercises with his mother and has not had an attack since.

Sometimes it takes weeks before any effect is noticed and at other times it's almost instant. Every child is so different. The intensity of improvement varies widely too, insofar as a problem can literally disappear overnight or slowly lessen over a period of time.

You will find that feedback from teachers can be very useful. One little girl was so timid at her new school that she hadn't said a word to anyone for weeks. Two days after being read "The

Princess" story, the teacher (who was not aware that the child had done the exercise) telephoned the parents to say, "what has happened to your daughter? She turned round and talked to the girl behind her in class today and I was so pleased to have to tell her that she must wait until break time".

Sometimes the changes in behaviour are very subtle, barely noticeable, and sometimes dramatic, but most children will derive some benefit from this work. The very least you will achieve is to further strengthen that very special bond that exists between you and your child and the satisfaction that you have helped your child on their way to reach his or her ultimate potential for a life of happiness.

What is quite remarkable is that the children somehow seem to know that the work is doing them good. One very disgruntled and furious young lady of 7 years said to her mother "My friends were really horrid to me at school today. Can we have The Princess story at bedtime and go and rescue a little girl who is very very angry."

Somehow the child knew that rescuing a little girl in her imagination would help her feel better about herself and what had upset her at school that day. And of course it illustrated to her mother the benefit of clearing out her daughter's repressions regularly, thus giving her child every opportunity to grow up to be the person that she was born to be, without the burden of those repressed emotions.

Can you imagine a world where there is no aggression, a world where teenagers do not turn to recreational drugs to induce excitement or to appease their anguish and confusion? I am always aware that today's children are tomorrow's parents and if we can start with this generation by guiding them to release their unconscious anxiety before the door to that repression store gets bolted, then we will have a generation of calm, harmonious adults. Our children will grow to become people who are lucid and balanced and have the ability to "live in the moment". Free of fear, able to cope with the problems of life and able to recognise and appreciate all the beauty and love of our existence.

Change cannot be forced upon society. Lasting, effective, change comes about via the efforts of individuals who are clear-minded, determined and have the interests of others at heart. In a small, but vitally important way, the process of repression-release in children could slowly, but surely, help bring about a harmonious and more balanced existence for a whole new generation.

CHAPTER 6

The Princess

Where you see (..........) insert your child's name

Let's pretend that you're a beautiful princess and that you live in a fairytale castle, just like the one in Disneyland. And this castle has turrets and towers, and at the very top of one of the towers there's a flag flying in the breeze. And there's a drawbridge that goes up and down across the water in the moat. And this castle is right in the middle of a magic forest, on the edge of a beautiful lake.

Sometimes you sit near the lake and watch all of the birds and animals come down for a drink. Hedgehogs and badgers and rabbits and squirrels. There's a lovely deer who brings her little baby deer down to the lake. It looks just like Bambi this little deer, and do you know what? It's getting to know you and trust you. Isn't that nice? He used to be scared of you, because he didn't know you, but now he knows that you're a lovely kind princess and he doesn't run away any more. I think that one day, very soon, he might let you get close enough to feed him. Won't that be good?

(Wait for response. A nod will do – just as long as she acknowledges the question.)

Now I want you to imagine that one day you're in your tower bedroom, and you're wearing a really beautiful dress. It sort of sparkles as you move. Oh, it's really lovely. And when you twirl around it flares out and floats around you. You can see it sparkling and twinkling as you watch yourself in the mirror.

You've got a really pretty silver crown on your head. It has points on it and each little point has a jewel at the top that sparkles and shimmers as you dance around the room in your satin slippers. Can you see yourself in the mirror? Don't you look beautiful?

Wait for child's response.

And I want you to pretend now that you dance over to the window to see if the little deer has arrived at the water's edge for his morning drink. No... he's not there yet; maybe it's a bit early for him. And as you're looking out of the tower window you can see the island in the middle of the lake. That island is a very special place. Because it belongs to you. You're so lucky: to have a special place that belongs just to you.

And as you're looking across that lovely golden lake to your island, you notice that something's different today. There's something on the island that you haven't noticed before. That's strange!!!!!! I wonder what it could be..... Shall we find out?

Wait for response

O.K. Now. I want you to imagine that you are setting off to find out. You go out of your bedroom and then down the stairs of the tower. That's right – down and down and down. All the way down to the bottom of the staircase and into the hall. Then down the steps into the courtyard. Then you go across the courtyard until you get to the entrance of the castle. The drawbridge is down, so you can cross the moat. And then you see the winding path that leads all the way down to the lake. And you stay on the path as it weaves and winds its way down towards the lake, going down and down. All the way down to the lake.

That's where you keep your boat - it's so beautiful! It's a golden boat and it has silken cushions for you to sit on., And guess what - it doesn't have sails, it's pulled along by a beautiful, pure white, swan. A very elegant, graceful, swan. She has a little coronet on her head to show everyone that she belongs to a princess. And whenever you want to ride in your boat you just tell her where you want to go, and she picks up the silver ribbons in her beak, the ones that are attached to the front of the boat, and she pulls the boat along behind her. Isn't that clever?

(Wait for response)

So now you step into the golden boat and make yourself comfortable on the silken cushions, and then you tell the swan that you'd like her to take you to your island please, and the beautiful, graceful, swan picks up the silver ribbons in her beak and begins to move off from the shore towards the middle of the lake. And as you glide across the smooth lake, you dip your hand into the water and watch the ripples spread out. It's a lovely warm day. The sky is really blue and you can see little fluffy clouds floating across the sky.

Very soon you come to the island, that

very special place that belongs to you. The swan pulls your boat to the edge of the jetty so that you can step out. Your island has a lovely beach – golden sand that stretches for miles and miles. And beautiful flowers and trees, and a meadow, right in the middle, where you sometimes go to pick the wild flowers. Then you ask the swan to wait right there for you while you make your way across the beach towards the meadow.

And as you get close to the meadow, you can see that there is something there that you haven't seen before. Lots of hot-air balloons. A long line of them. Now...I don't know what colour these balloons are, but very soon you'll be amazed to discover that they can become any colour that you want them to be. Each balloon has a strong woven basket below it, and is anchored to the ground with a very strong, very thick, rope.

And nearby is a table, and on the table

are lots of tins of paint, all different colours, every colour you can ever imagine, and there's a big box of brand new paintbrushes.

And I want you to notice the other things that are there too. On the ground there is a great big toolbox that's just filled to the brim with all sorts of tools – saws and chisels, hammers, drills, spanners, nuts and bolts – all the things you could possibly need. And there's a stepladder too.

You're just beginning to wonder what all of this is doing on your island, when suddenly, you hear a fluttering noise above you, and you look up, expecting to see a bird overhead, but it's not a bird. It's a piece of paper. A piece of paper floating down and down towards you, drifting down on a gentle breeze, swaying first to the left, and then to the right, and then swirling round and round in a circle, but all the time, getting closer and closer to you, until finally it lands at your feet.

And I want you to imagine that you bend down to pick it up, and you notice that it's addressed to you, it's addressed to Princess (.........) Isn't that amazing?

(Wait for child's nod or reply)

And you read it, and then you know. It says you have a very important mission to perform here. You're going to rescue a little girl who needs your help. And guess what? This little girl's name is the same as yours! Isn't that funny? Now this little (..............) is feeling very uncomfortable, really really sad, and you're going to make her feel better. You're going to show her how to get rid of those horrible feelings. That will cheer her up, won't it?

(Wait for nod)

Now, I want you to go around the meadow to look for that little girl called (............) who feels really unhappy, a sad little (............) who was so unhappy and forlorn. I don't know what could have made her so sad, but I do know that she'll be very glad to get rid of that feeling, won't she?

(Wait for nod)

I wonder what colour "sad" would be if it had to be a colour. What do you think? What colour do you suppose it might be?

(Await answer. Suppose the child says "yellow")

Yellow! Mmmmmmmmmm! That sounds just right for a sad feeling. O.K. So now go round the meadow looking for that little girl, that little (............) who's so sad and unhappy. You'll recognise her very easily because she'll be all filled up with that yellow feeling, that uncomfortable, sad, unhappy, feeling. You just let me know when you've found her. Take your time, there's no hurry.

O.K. I've got her (or similar response).

Wonderful. Now... I want you to explain to her about your mission, that you've come to find her so that you can take away that horrible feeling, that sad, yellow, feeling. You don't have to say it out loud, just let me know when you've told her that, when you are sure that she understands.

O.K. I've told her.

Good. Alright now, take her by the hand and lead her over to the line of balloons. That's right. And when you reach the line of balloons, I want you to find the yellow paint. Then both of you take a paintbrush each and, between you, start to paint the first balloon with the yellow paint. And the basket underneath it. One of you can use the stepladder to get to the top of the balloon. Or perhaps you can take it in turns. Off you go now and let me know when you've done that.

We've finished.

That's brilliant. You're doing really well. Now you've got some more work to do. I want you, between you, to load all of that yellow feeling out of (............) and into the basket. Make sure you get it all, every last bit of that horrible sad, unhappy, yellow feeling. Pile it all into the basket. Every bit of it.

We've done it.

Great. Now..... Have a look in the toolbox and each of you find something to cut through that thick rope. Tell me what you've chosen.

We've got a saw with a handle both ends so that we can work together (Or whatever)

O.K. Away you go. Saw through that thick rope and let me know when you get through to the very last strand.

We've done it, we've cut through it.

That's the way !!!! That's really good. Now.... Both of you, hold hands really tightly and watch that yellow balloon begin to rise up. Very very slowly at first, then getting higher and higher and higher. It's as high as the tree tops now. And still going higher. Up as high as the fluffy clouds now, and even higher, soaring higher and higher. Now it's just a tiny speck in the distance, you can hardly see it. Now it's floated up through the earth's atmosphere, higher than the sun, higher than the stars, and it's drifted off into space. Never to be seen again.

Wow!!! Have a look at little (............)'s face. Tell me what you see.

She's smiling.

That's wonderful. What a great team! She's so pleased to have got rid of that feeling. Give her a big hug. A really big one, that's right. And tell her that you're really proud of her.

And now hold her hand again and take her to where the swan is waiting with the beautiful golden boat. And help the little girl into the boat and make her comfy on the cushions.

Then you tell the swan that you'd like to go back to the castle please, and you watch as the swan picks up the silver ribbons and begins to pull the boat away from the island. The little girl is so amazed. She's never seen a swan pulling a boat before. She is having such a wonderful time and she is so pleased that you came to rescue her, so that she can be with you.

Now you're gliding across the sparkling clear lake, back towards the castle. And as you get closer and closer to the shore you can see something right at the edge of the water.

It's that little baby deer. He looks really pleased to see you coming. He's been waiting for you. He lifts up his head and watches as you and the little girl get out of the boat. And as you go towards him, he's not a bit afraid. And he starts walking slowly towards you. He wants to be friends – isn't that nice? Now all of you will be able to play together and have lots of adventures.

And you'll be able to teach the little girl so many things. How to draw with coloured pencils. How to brush her hair and clean her teeth. How to pick wild flowers and put them in a vase. How to make a daisy chain to hang around the little deer's neck.

I don't know what kind of games you'd like to play – maybe hide and seek.

What do you think....................."

(At this point the work is completed and it is now up to you to either continue on with your own and your child's input, or bring the story to an end).

CHAPTER 7

The Captain

Where you see (..........) insert your child's name

Let's pretend that you're a forest ranger – you're a captain in the rangers, and you live in a big fort in the middle of a beautiful forest. And this fort is right next to a lake. You're in charge of all of the rangers who live in the fort. You have to inspect your rangers every day to make sure that they're spick and span in their smart uniforms. Their uniforms are really smart, but not as smart as yours, because you're the captain.

And you have to teach the rangers all sorts of things like how to fish and hunt for food, how to take care of themselves as well as looking after the wildlife. The rangers sleep in the barracks, but you have your very own room in the tower at the corner, because you're the captain and you need to keep an eye on things.

I want you to imagine that one day you're in your room and you are cleaning your boots. You've made such a good job of them. They are so shiny that you can see your face in them. And then you get dressed in your uniform and then put on your boots. You look really cool. And then you reach for your comb and smarten yourself up, put on your hat with its shiny badge and look into the mirror and see yourself. Don't you look well-groomed and smart? Can you see yourself in the mirror?

(Wait for nod or response)

And now you go over to the window and look out across the lake. You can see an island right in the middle of the lake. It's a very special place, this island, because it belongs to you. It's your very own special place. You're the only person that's ever allowed there.

But today, you notice that something's different – there's something on the island that you haven't noticed before. So you decide to investigate. Imagine now that you go out of your room, and then down the stairs of the tower, all the way down, down and down, and round and round. All the way down to the bottom, and then out into the courtyard. Then you go across the yard and the rangers salute you as you go through the big wooden gate. Now you look for the path that leads all the way down to the shore of the lake. And just stay on that path as it leads you down and down towards the lake.

That's where you keep your boat. It's a very smart sailing boat with white sails, and you set the sails, and then the wind begins to fill the sails and you start to move .... and away you go. Sailing across the smooth lake, just like the fluffy white clouds sailing across the blue sky. You have your hand on the tiller so that you can steer the way, and very soon you come to the island.

You steer your way until the boat is alongside the jetty. You're really good at that, guiding yourself to where you want to be. Then you pick up the rope and jump out of the boat on to the jetty. You have to tie the rope to a pole so that the boat doesn't float away.

It's really lovely on your island, that very special place that belongs to you. There's miles and miles of golden sand and in the middle of the island there is a meadow with lots of trees and flowers. And you go across the beach towards the meadow. You can hear the sound of the birds calling to each other.

And as you get close to the meadow, you can see a long line of hot air balloons. Now...I don't know what colour these balloons are, but very soon you'll be amazed to discover that they can become any colour that you want them to be. Each balloon has a strong woven basket below it, and each one is anchored to the ground with a very strong, very thick, rope.

And I want you to notice the other things there too. On the ground is a large tool-box that's just filled to the brim with all sorts of tools – saws and chisels, hammers, files, spanners, nuts and bolts – all the things you could possibly need. And there's a stepladder there too.

And nearby is a table, and on the table are lots of tins of paint, all different colours, every colour you can ever imagine, and there's a big box of brand new paintbrushes.

You are just beginning to wonder what all of this is doing on your island, when suddenly, you hear a fluttering noise above you, and you look up, expecting to see a bird overhead, but it's not a bird. It's a piece of paper. A piece of paper floating down towards you, drifting down on a gentle breeze, fluttering to the left, and then to the right, and then swirling round in a circle, but all the time, getting closer and closer to you, until finally it lands at your feet.

And you bend down to pick it up, and you notice that it's addressed to you, it's addressed to Captain (.........). Isn't that amazing?

(Wait for child's nod or reply)

And you read it, and then you know. It says that you have a very important mission to perform here. You're going to find a little boy who needs your help. And, do you know, he has the same name as you. Isn't that funny? Now, this little boy is feeling very uncomfortable, really really sad and unhappy, and you're going to make him feel better. You're going to get rid of those horrible feelings for him. That will cheer him up, won't it?

(Wait for nod)

Now, first of all, I want you to look for that little boy called (............) who's feeling really unhappy, a sad little (............) who's so unhappy and forlorn. I don't know what could have made him so sad, but I do know that he'll be very glad to get rid of that feeling, won't he?

(Wait for nod)

I wonder what colour "sad" would be if it had to be a colour. What do you think? What colour do you suppose it might be?

(Await response. Suppose the child says "yellow")

Yellow! Mmmmmmmmmm! That sounds just right for a sad feeling. O.K. So now go round the meadow looking for that little boy, that little (............) who is so sad and unhappy. You'll recognise him very easily because he'll be all filled up with that horrible yellow feeling, that uncomfortable, sad, feeling. You just let me know when you've found him. Take your time, there's no hurry.

O.K. I've got him (or similar response).

Wonderful. Now...I want you to explain to him about your mission, that you've come to find him so that you can take away that horrible feeling, that sad, yellow, feeling. You don't have to say it out loud, just let me know when you've told him that, when you are really sure he understands.

O.K. I've told him.

Well done. All right now, take him by the hand and lead him over to the line of balloons. That's right. And when you reach the line of balloons, I want you to find the tin of yellow paint, then take a paintbrush each from the box and, between you, paint the balloon yellow. And the basket underneath it. Paint it all yellow. One of you will have to go up the ladder to reach the top of the balloon, or maybe you can take it in turns. Let me know when you've done that.

We've finished.

You're doing really well. Now, you've got some more work to do. I want you, between you, to load all of that sad, unhappy, yellow feeling out of (..............) and into the yellow basket. Pile it all into the basket. Every bit of it. And let me know when you've done that.

O.K. We've done it.

Brilliant!! Now, have a look in the toolbox and each of you find something to cut through the rope. Tell me what you've chosen.

We've got an axe each (or whatever).

O.K. Away you go then. Chop through that thick rope. Let me know when you get to the very last strand.

We've done it. We've cut through it.

Yeah!!!!!!! That's the way! Now... Both of you - hold hands. Watch that yellow balloon begin to rise up. Very, very, slowly at first, then getting higher and higher and higher. Up as high as the treetops now. Now it's as high as the birds fly, and it's going even higher. It's as high as the fluffy clouds, and even higher, soaring higher and higher. Now it's a tiny speck in the distance and gone forever. Up through the earth's atmosphere and drifting off into space. Never to be seen again.

Wow!!! Have a look at little (............)'s face. Tell me what you see.

He's smiling.

That's wonderful. What a great team! He's so pleased to have got rid of that feeling. - give him a really big hug. A really big one, that's right. Tell him how proud you are of him.

Now hold his hand again and take him to the shore where you left the boat. Help him into the boat, and then set the sails to take you back to the fort. Now you can untie the rope and push off from the jetty. Now the boat is moving out across the lake, gliding across the sparkling clear water, back towards the fort. The sun is shining and the sky is very blue with little white fluffy clouds. And you feel so happy because you rescued that little boy. You're a real hero.

He thinks that you're ever so clever to be able to sail a boat and you can explain to him what all the different ropes are for and how the tiller works. He really wants to learn. Then as you get close to the shore, near where the fort is, he helps you to pull in the sails and you glide alongside the jetty and he helps you to tie up the boat.

You have so much to teach him. You can take him to the forest and show him how to look for animal tracks. And where all the animals come down to the lake for a drink. And where the eagles nest, and where the deer hide in the forest. And you can teach him how to fish and how to swim, and how to be a ranger, and look after the wild life, just like you do. Because you're the captain and you know all about these things. You'll have such a lot of fun together. What do you think you'll like doing best...................?"

(At this point the work is completed and it is now up to you to either continue on with your own and your child's input, or bring the story to an end).

CHAPTER 8

Variations

For all children

In the script we have used the term "sad and unhappy" to describe a particular feeling and I suggest that the first time you read this story to your child you use this term because it covers a multitude of emotions.

However, there will be times when you will know exactly what is bothering your child and I have listed below some of the other feelings that children repress. I am sure that you will discover many more. These can be substituted for the "sad and unhappy" term used in the script. For instance, if you know that your child is feeling particularly nervous about starting a new school, then the term "frightened" could be used instead, or maybe "worried". Bear in mind that you should not say "frightened at school" only "frightened". **Remember the secret at all times**. It is vital that we never ever mention what we know is troubling the child.

Angry	Guilty
Lonely	Embarrassed
Frightened	Poorly
Jealous	Hateful
Unloved	Worried
Left Out	Confused
Nervous	Hurt
Misunderstood	Not good enough
Intimidated	Unwanted
Anxious	Insecure
Doesn't fit in	Naughty

Obviously, younger children will not understand some of those words, so it will be necessary for you to use terminology that you know your child understands.

You can embellish and embroider to your heart's content and add your own comments, which should be said just before the Princess or the Captain goes looking round the meadow. For instance, when dealing with the "guilty" feeling you could say "Perhaps she's (he's) been a bit naughty and feels uncomfortable. She (he) doesn't know that it's all forgiven and forgotten now, and there's nothing more to worry about."

Some children really do believe that in order for a parent to love someone new, like a step-parent or a step-sibling, that it is necessary for the natural parent to take love away from that child to give to the newcomer. So, when dealing with the "jealous" feeling it would be useful to say something like "Maybe that little girl/boy who is feeling jealous doesn't understand that when someone new comes into a person's life to love, they don't have to take love away from the people who they already love. Truly, they still love them just as much. You see, hearts are made of elastic. The more people who come into someone's life to love, the bigger the heart gets, so then there's love enough and room enough for everybody."

It would be very easy to assume that children are too young to have a large capacity to hate.

I made that mistake whilst I was doing a version of "The Captain" story with a boy in his early teens. I asked him if there was any other boy in the meadow who had a feeling that we hadn't dealt with and he practically spat out the word "hate". When it came to the part where he had to load the horrible black hate feeling into the basket he said "can we use two balloons for this, there's so much of it?" Incidentally, this boy had the most incredible result after this particular exercise and changed so much that his parents could scarcely believe it.

I have found it a rewarding privilege to work with children, and it is extremely eye-opening. They are natural actors and actresses and really get into the spirit of the exercises. I was once working with a little girl who had chosen the colour green for "guilty". She was quite a while finding the little girl in the meadow and then whispered to me very conspiratorially "Sorry I was so long – she was hiding behind a bush".

When you have been using the exercises for a while you can extend the scope of the story by saying "is there any other little girl (boy) in the meadow that has an uncomfortable feeling? A feeling that we don't know about?" Your child might want to tell you what that feeling is, or might want to keep it undisclosed. It is not a good idea to force the issue. You could simply say "She (he) doesn't have to say what it is. You know what to do to rescue her (him), so I'll sit here very quietly while you go and do that and you just let me know when you're finished." Then carry on with the story when your child is ready.

Although I am sure you would like to know exactly what horrible feeling is bothering your child, bear in mind that as your child becomes stronger and more confident as a result of these exercises, she (he) will gain the self-assurance to tell you more.

There is absolutely no reason why you shouldn't vary the stories to suit your child. It is the work on the island that is important, and that is the section that should be read to them exactly as the script reads. For instance, if you have an older boy who is keen on cars you could make up a story about his favourite car. He can collect it from the showroom and go off for a drive. Make the story go on for a while, and then he comes to the top of hill where he stops and parks the car. He can look down into the valley and see a large lake with an island in the middle...

Or for an older girl. Well, she could be a film actress perhaps, and go on location to a castle beside a lake. She could be trying on various clothes in her room and seeing herself in the mirror.....

You know your own child best and I am sure you will find the best way for you both. The things to incorporate in your story are as follows:-

1. Make sure you have the child's attention and keep it going by asking them questions that they need to respond to from time to time. For instance "can you see yourself in the mirror?" Or "Shall we find out?".....

2. Use the expressions "down and down – all the way down" a few times in the first part of your story. This will help to get your child's attention focused inwards and the imagination will step up a gear.

3. Have them look into a mirror for some reason. The boys could adjust their rear-view mirror in their cars and the girls could be dressing up and then see themselves in a mirror. This will help the child to become more self-aware, even though we are (ostensibly) dealing with a different child in the story.

4. This point is very important: the child is going "to a very special place that belongs to you. Your very own special place". Saying this will get the children to focus on the very centre of their inner self, which is where we need to reach in order to bring about the desired changes.

For younger children

At the point in the script where the balloon begins to rise up from the ground, ask your child to start it off by blowing at it (and you can join in too to give some encouragement). This is a wonderful way to get more participation from your child, and thus a better result.

It would be perfect if you could get the child to take a few good deep breaths before you begin the story. Saying something like "let's get lots of air into us before we start, because I know there are balloons in this story and we'll want to do lots of blowing," might do the trick.

CHAPTER 9

Frequently asked questions

- *How often should I do the exercises with my little girl?*

That very much depends on your daughter, but I would suggest that once a week would be an ideal starting point until any problem she has clears itself, and after that, whenever you feel it necessary. One thing to bear in mind is that some children become very tired after the exercises. It takes quite a lot of physical energy to do the work, even though your child is lying down and it might seem as though nothing much is happening.

Some children tend to wake later the following morning too.

• *How long does the effect last?*

This is very difficult to judge because children are repressing all the time and it is possible that whatever is troubling your child will continue to cause repressions to take place. Let us take as an example the little girl who was the first child to use the Princess story. She lived in a somewhat dysfunctional family where alcohol and drug abuse was prevalent; not only in her immediate family, but also in her extended family of cousins, aunts and uncles who lived nearby. The child would therefore have witnessed erratic and irresponsible behaviour from some of the adults in her world. Although she stopped wetting the bed after just one Princess exercise it is possible that, if she continued to witness more violent arguments between her parents, then more anxiety would repress into her subconscious mind and the bed-wetting would start up again. This work can only clear out the emotion that is already in the repression store. It cannot prevent more repressions taking place. (Thank goodness – we have no wish to interfere with the wonderful process of repression and so deprive children of their superbly efficient defence mechanism. Children will always repress: it is their salvation.) So if a problem in the family is ongoing then regular "clear-outs" would be necessary.

• *Up to what age is this work suited?*
For as long as you can get the child to willingly participate in the story. If you can keep it going until your child is 16, then the door will bolt on an empty repression chamber. You will consequently have a very well adjusted teenager who will grow into a fulfilled and balanced adult. I have even had colleagues tell me that they have successfully used this technique on their adult clients, and, whilst it would by no means take the place of a programme of adult analysis, it does sometimes reach a few repressions that are not too deeply buried. In passing, I would mention here that, unlike children, when adults release their repressions it is often accompanied by tears. One or more parent is always present when I am treating their child and they, too, are asked to

close their eyes whilst we work. Quite often I hear a sob from behind me and turn round to find the mother with a tear streaked face. So ladies, if you want to practice "The Princess on each other, it might be a good idea to have a few tissues handy before you start. And if you want to get the very best out of it, have the "receiver" spend a few minutes breathing really deeply before you start.

• *You say at the end of Chapter 8, "for younger children". Up to what age are you referring?*

Use it for as long as you can. If you can get a child of 10+ to "blow" at the balloon as it takes off, then do so. It really does help the process enormously. You could join in too to give some encouragement. The harder they work, the better the result. Some children will think it too babyish and won't want to try, whilst others are more biddable and won't question it.

• *Is this work suitable for all children, even those who do not have a particular problem?*

Absolutely. If every child had an empty repression store when the door bolts at the age of 16, then their behaviour and the way in which it would affect life for them and their families would be far more agreeable. It is no coincidence that youngsters can go wild in their teens. Not only are their newly acquired hormones changing their bodies at a rapid rate and also affecting their emotions, but to add to this the door is bolting fast on their repressions. What a predicament! Imagine all those bubbles now! They are trapped. You can almost hear them yelling "let me out, let me out". They are making a last-ditch attempt to be free by trying to discharge the trapped negative energy. Buried childhood repressions go a long way towards explaining teenage aggression and bad behaviour.

- *Is it possible to work with more than one child at a time?*

Unfortunately not. This work is designed to enable each child to utilise their imagination and to participate to the fullest extent and it is this individual participation that makes it such a powerful process. However, even though you may have to juggle bedtime routines, I am certain that you will find it worthwhile to do so.

• *Is it necessary to do the stories at bedtime?*
It is the optimum time because the subconscious mind uses the sleep period to do its filing and restructuring. There is no reason why you cannot do the stories at any time at all, but just before sleep would add to the potency of the work.

• *We've tried so many different ways to help my nine-year-old son with his lack of confidence, taking him to many places for help. He's getting more and more desperate and keeps asking us to find a way to help him. Can't we tell him that this work will help?*
Absolutely not. Not before you work with him, nor during, nor afterwards. By telling him that this work will help him, you will not be helping him at all, in fact, quite the opposite. You will be hindering him by putting more pressure on his conscious mind to succeed. Remember, these

exercise are designed for working through the unconscious mind whilst the child is not even aware that he is being helped.

• *How on earth do I get my older child to co-operate?* This is a tricky one! I have never experienced the problem because when a child is brought to me, even older teenagers, they do exactly as I ask them to, without question. Having said that, it is invariably mums and dads who carry out the exercises at home with their child that get a better and quicker result than I do. If you feel that your child is too old to listen to a story, why not say instead that it's a relaxation exercise? As long as you don't say something like "this will cure your aggressive behaviour" or "this will stop you being afraid of the dark".

In other words, on no account should you make any reference to a specific problem, or even that one exists at all.

I can give you an example of a father who was at his wit's end because his son was on the point of being expelled from school because of aggressive behaviour. The teenage boy lived with his mother and her new partner and the father saw his son every other weekend. He gave his son a choice: "I have talked this over with your mother and we are in total agreement. We have found a way to help you relax. It sounds a bit strange, but we've heard that it works. Either you cooperate or you are grounded for 6 months. The father made up a story where the boy flew a micro-light aeroplane to the island because his son loved aircraft and had always wanted to be a pilot. It worked a treat!

• *Suppose my child falls asleep during the story?*
No problem. A goodnight kiss then creep out of the room. Try again another time.

• *Can The Princess and The Ranger stories be used for any age at all, even older teenagers?*
Yes. Even for adults, as I mentioned earlier. We all have a small child somewhere inside of ourselves and that part of us will respond to the make-believe aspect of the story. As explained in the

variations section, the vital work takes place on the island. How you get your child to arrive at the island really doesn't matter as long as you adhere to the instructions given in the variations chapter, and they are actively involved in making the transition to their innermost minds (represented by the island).

CHAPTER 10

So is it really just that simple?
You tell me!

Amazingly, it really is as simple as I have described. The stories are no more than a pleasant means of opening the door and reaching the innermost part of your child's mind.

Remember, our unconscious minds work symbolically. There is no sense of logic, reason or time within that part of our minds, even when we become adults. It is the symbolism of the work carried out on the island that will release the trapped energy caused by repressed emotions. When this negativity is released, the problems caused by that trapped emotion simply float away, just like the balloons in the story. There is no energy for the problem to feed on any more. And that's all there is to it.

I have infinite faith in the power and the instincts of motherhood and consequently have no doubt that you will find many additional ways to build on the methods contained within these pages. We have been telling our children bedtime stories since time began, using our imagination to colour their worlds and expand their awareness and knowledge. By this process we also teach them how to use their own imagination too, giving them the opportunity to reach into those worlds that lie outside their own experience.

When you have used the methods contained within these pages and can see the positive changes in your children for yourself, you might wish to share your experiences to help other parents achieve the same results. For example, with your approval, the results you achieve could be used in revised editions of this book. There is always room for further knowledge and experience in our quest for bestowing upon our children the very best that we can give.

I wish you happy story-telling (and don't forget to keep the secret!)

Whilst it is not possible for the author to enter into personal correspondence, she would be pleased to hear from you by writing to her via her publishers:

> evolutionary pathways
> P.O. Box 8121
> Billericay
> CM11 1WZ

Or by e-mail at: info@stress-busting.com

Further copies of this book may be ordered direct from the author's website at:

www.stress-busting.com

Acknowledgements

I would like to express my grateful thanks to the following people. In particular to my husband, David, whose wisdom and patience kept me focussed on the task in hand, as well as providing invaluable help in all of the practical issues involved. Without the loving support and encouragement from both him and from Katie Miles, this book would not have been written.

I would also like to thank Jerry Robertson, Nic Jones, Molly Callender and Jeremy Scott for the time and guidance they so generously provided.